That scene has stayed in my mind and took place about 200 kilometres from where I live now. It is in Kosovo, where I was brought up. Now I live in Vrnjacka Banja, in central Serbia.

My background is Orthodox. I don't remember my mother ever visiting a church but my father, who was a roadman, went about once a year. However, as far as I know, he never entered the church. There was an event there at Christmas or Easter time and he stood outside the celebration along with all the others who did not go inside. He was not very interested in the ceremony, just in being nearby.

# Not Even One

In 1956, when I was seven years old, I went to school. I liked it even when we had to travel there in deep snow in winter. I didn't have good shoes but despite that I enjoyed school, even with cold, wet feet. When I was a child, religion was something that was for the past and there was a totally materialistic view of the world. The slogan we learned was 'There is no God.' I grew up knowing no Bible stories at all, not even one. I may have seen crucifixes on some historic monasteries but they meant nothing to me, they were just to do with old and pointless traditions.

# Holidays and Celebrations

Once a year we had a holiday on a saint's day and we had to take special bread called Slava cake to the priest to be placed in my home village of Ljevosa. The saint was St John, Slava, and his day was the 20th of January. I was given a little money to take for the priest's dedication of Slava cake. That was my job. As a child we celebrated Christmas but only with special food. It was not a religious celebration, nothing to do with the birth of Christ. It was the same at Easter. We had painted eggs but didn't know they had anything to do with Jesus rising from the dead.

# Deep Thoughts

Although we were told nothing about Jesus, in my mind I was thinking about things. It was while I was in elementary school that I started thinking that there must be something eternal. I thought a lot about eternity at that time. I had nobody to teach me and no Bible to read but in my mind I imagined that there must be an eternity and an opposite of eternity. I saw people were dying and my question all the time was – we are here for a time and then there is the end so what about eternity? I seemed to know that eternity is time without end. That was a burden to me at the time because I didn't know how to find an answer.

At that time there were all kind of diseases that children caught. My mother told me that I had six brothers and sisters whom I never saw. They had died in infancy before I was born. Perhaps it was knowing about my dead brothers and sisters that put thoughts of eternity into my mind, when I was too young to really think about these things.

# Big Decisions

School was strict. The teacher disciplined us by hitting us on the hands with a special stick. The teacher even ordered her wooden stick from my mother and I was obliged to take it to the classroom. With that stick I was often struck and I didn't like it. It was normal and accepted at that time but I'm glad to say that it does not happen now.

In middle school I studied economics. I also learned to touch type without looking. I was good at that work. We had eight years of elementary school and then middle school for four years. After that came the time to make big decisions about life.

# Searching for Truth

I was still troubled about eternity and I started drinking and listening to loud music. Maybe I was trying to suppress the voice from inside with its questions about what came after life and death – questions to which I still had no answers. It was in 1966 when, with my friends and relatives, I went on a visit home to Ljevosa. There I met my cousin, Simo Ralevic, who had recently become a believer in Jesus Christ. I think he might have been in theological school by then. He was nine years older than me.

We started a Bible study and that was when I first saw a New Testament. From 1966 to 1968 I went to the Bible study from time to time, not often. Although I was still not a Christian, I would argue against those who opposed Christianity. At one Bible study the subject was time, eternity and the end of time. It was so graphic that it hit my stony heart and mind hard enough for them to open and for me to understand. I saw eternity and Jesus in the centre of that eternity. Then the Holy Spirit brought about my conversion which I simply experienced as a moving from above. All that combined to help me to understand about eternity and Jesus Christ and the reason for his birth, death and resurrection.

# A Great Joy

After that I could say with great conviction and joy to my friend Cedo, 'From now I am a Christian.' And I remember the words he said. 'You know Dragisa, now the angels in heaven are rejoicing.' For me, a nineteen-year-old, there was a great joy to know that the angels were rejoicing.

When I told my parents that I had become a Christian, my father was just silent. I think he was converted because he was never opposed to it and he read the Bible.

My mother, in the beginning, liked what happened in my life and was not against it. She prepared food when Simo came to celebrate my conversion. Later she opposed my baptism but before she died, at the age of ninety-three, I explained the way of salvation, and she said that she believed.

# Jesus is the Way

I started my eighteen months' army service the same month I was converted. Yugoslavia was a communist state. Atheism and evolution were taught in schools. Men had evolved from monkeys and faith in God was ridiculed. The Bible was a forbidden book, especially if you were in the army. I had a small New Testament that I put in my pocket. After eighteen months it had left a stamp on the lining of my pocket but it was never found. The punishment would have been harsh if it had been.

From time to time – not often – I could secretly read some verses. The page where Jesus says 'I am the way, the truth and the life' (John 14:6) was one of my favourites. I was just at the very beginning of my new life as a Christian but I knew I had found the truth. I remember this very clearly.

(Based on *I am Mr Dragisa* – the story of Dragisa Armus and Blythswood Serbia, first published in *Wonderful: Blythswood People Share Stories of God's Faithfulness* by Irene Howat, Christian Focus Publications, 2016.)

# Eternity and Solomon

*For everything there is a season,
and a time for every matter under heaven:
a time to be born, and a time to die;
a time to plant, and a time to pluck up what is planted;
a time to kill, and a time to heal;
a time to break down, and a time to build up;
a time to weep, and a time to laugh;
a time to mourn, and a time to dance;
a time to cast away stones, and a time to gather stones together;
a time to embrace, and a time to refrain from embracing;
a time to seek, and a time to lose;
a time to keep, and a time to cast away;
a time to tear, and a time to sew;
a time to keep silence, and a time to speak;
a time to love, and a time to hate;
a time for war, and a time for peace.*

*What gain has the worker from his toil? I have seen the business that God has given to the children of man to be busy with. He has made everything beautiful in its time. Also, he has put eternity into man's heart, yet so that he cannot find out what God has done from the beginning to the end.*

(Ecclesiastes 3:1-11. ESV. Ecclesiastes is one of the books of the Bible and is believed to have been written by Solomon, king in Jerusalem.)

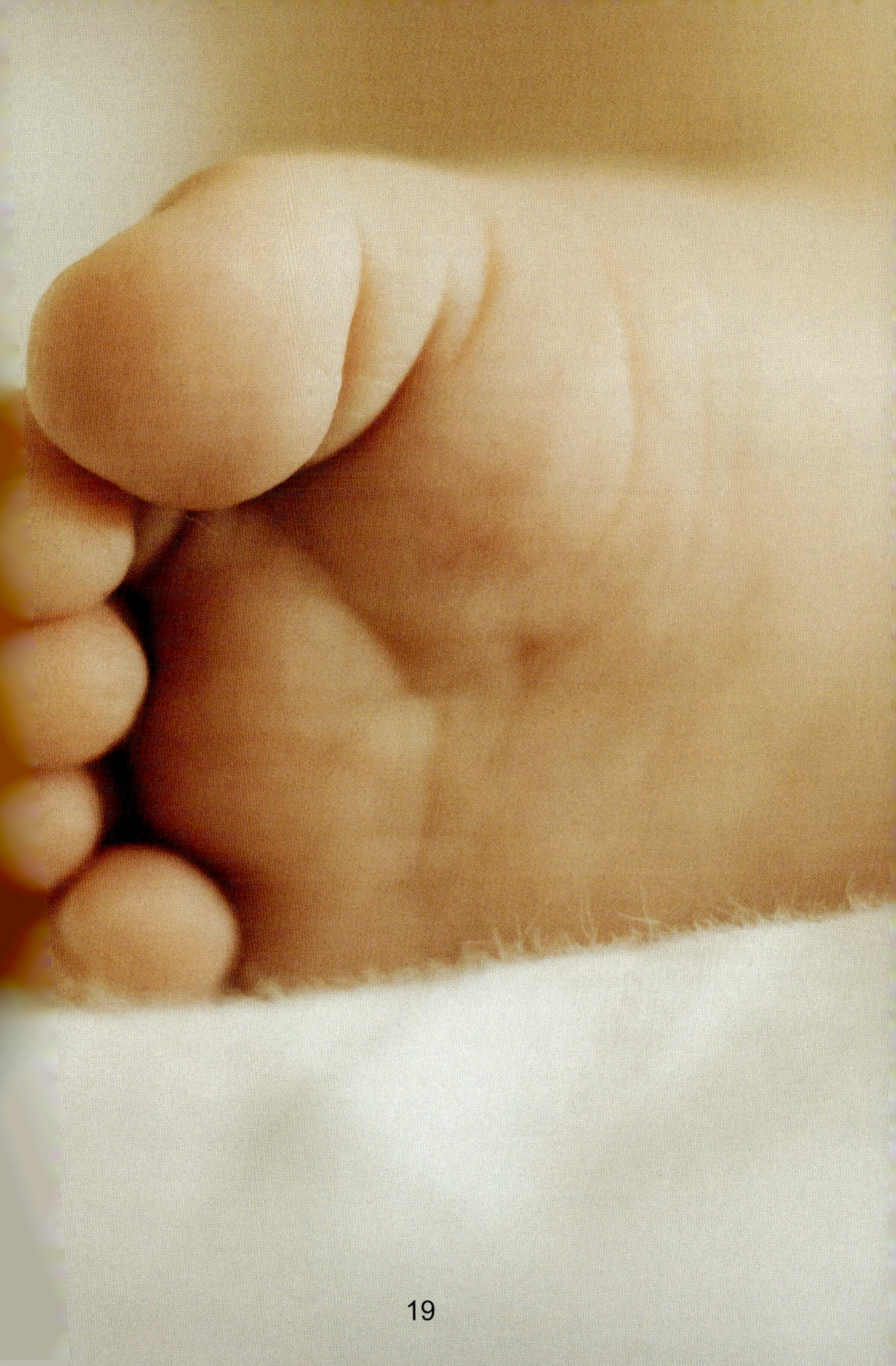

# Eternity and You

God has put eternity in every heart. Solomon was a wise man. He observed the transience of time and he was not happy. Wealth, fame, pleasure – all these things he enjoyed as a king but they did not bring him real satisfaction. He discovered that to experience joy, happiness and purpose in life he must be ready for eternity. This was his conclusion: *Fear God and keep his commandments, because this applies to every person.*

To have eternal life we must obey God's rules. But we have broken them! We all have sinned and wandered away from God. We need to turn away from sin and turn to God. How can we do this? Only by faith in Jesus Christ who came into this world to save us.

The name Jesus means 'Saviour'. Sometimes he is called Emmanuel which means God with us. Listen carefully to these great words that explain why the God of eternity has sent to us his Son:

Photographs: Dragisa Armus

*For God so loved the world, that he gave his only begotten Son, that whoever believes in him should not perish but have eternal life. (John 3:16)*

What a wonderful message! This is Good News for you and for me and for everyone who will believe in Jesus.

The question of eternity is in your heart: How can I have eternal life? Do not suppress it. Find the answer. The answer is Jesus. If you believe in Jesus, you have eternal life. He loved you. He gave his life for you. He forgives your sins and makes you right with God. He gives you real purpose in life and lasting joy. Believe in the Lord Jesus Christ and you will be saved!

# Blythswood Care

## Education, Community, Gospel

Working from its base in the Highlands of Scotland, Blythswood Care is transforming the lives of children and adults in Europe, Africa and Asia. Education is one primary goal, bringing opportunities to disadvantaged children and young people. Community is another, with projects that extend help to people marginalised by poverty or prejudice. Gospel underpins both objectives, giving practical expression to the Christian beliefs that have motivated this organisation for more than 50 years.

Blythswood assists Christians and non-Christians alike, believing that everyone is precious in God's sight. Blythswood shares the gospel at every opportunity, believing it is for everyone – *For God so loved the world, that he gave his only Son, that whoever believes in him should not perish but have eternal life.* (John 3:16, ESV)

Head Office: Highland Deephaven, Evanton, Ross-shire Scotland, IV16 9XJ

www.blythswood.org

Scottish charity SC048001

info@blythswood.org